The Royal Spy

The Royal Spy

Ayesha Braganza
Fathima Hakkim

Collins

Contents

Noor-Un-Nisa Inayat Khan's family tree

(children)
|
Maula Bakhsh ———— Qasim Bi
|
Rahmat Khan ——— Khadija Bibi
(1843–1910)   (1868–1902)

Hazrat Inayat Khan
(1882–1927)

Noor-Un-Nisa Inayat Khan
(1914–1944)

Vilayat Khan
(1916–2004)

2

Tipu Sultan (Fath Ali Khan), Tiger of Mysore
(1750–1799)

Ruler of the Kingdom of Mysore 1782–1799

Ora Ray Baker
(1888–1949)

Hidayat Khan
(1917–2016)

Khair-Un-Nisa Khan
(1919–2011)

Noor's journey

1917 the family moves from London to Paris

1942 Noor flies into France

1940 the family escape Paris and drive to Tours

they board a boat at Le Verdon and sail to Falmouth

they travel by train to Bordeaux

FALMOUTH

LONDON

BEAULIEU

PARIS

TOURS

LE VERDON

BORDEAUX

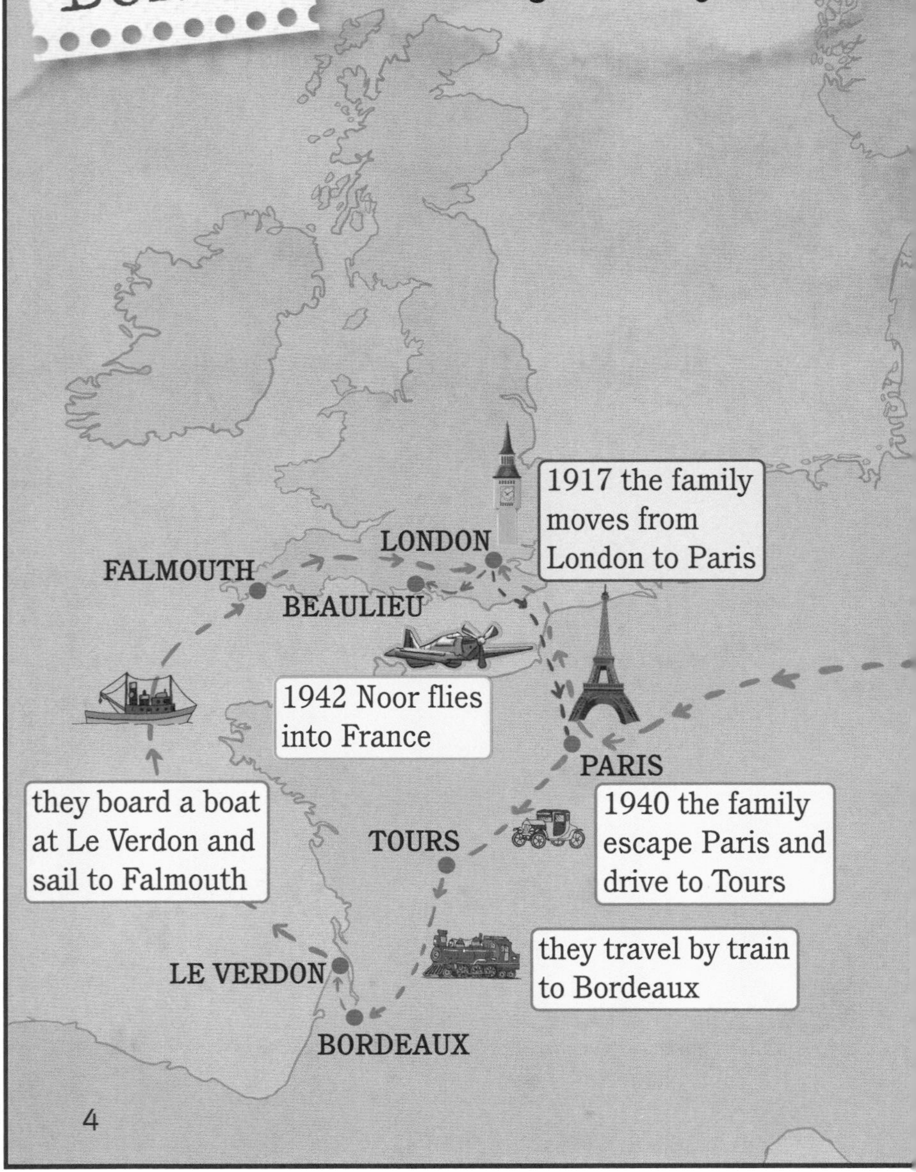

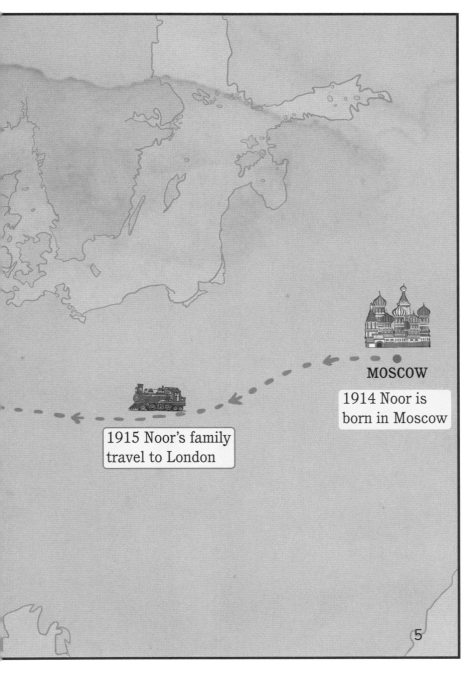

MOSCOW

1914 Noor is born in Moscow

1915 Noor's family travel to London

Young Noor

This is Noor-Un-Nisa Inayat Khan as a young girl. Nothing in this image suggests that Noor would grow up to be a spy. Many stories about spies give us the idea that they are all strong, sporty men. Noor was an imaginative, musical girl who wasn't particularly sporty. Her story shows us that spies can come from the most unexpected places.

Princess Noor

Noor's background was fascinating. She was mixed heritage with an Indian father and an American mother. The story of her father's background might explain where Noor got her courage, which was one of the many qualities that made her such a fantastic spy.

Noor's great-great-great grandfather was the Indian Muslim ruler, Tipu Sultan. This made Noor a princess.

Tipu Sultan was the ruler of the Kingdom of Mysore.

Courageous royalty

Tipu Sultan was the king of a part of India called Mysore. He fought against the British who were trying to **colonise** India at this time. His courage and bravery in fighting earned him the name "Tiger of Mysore". Noor shared this quality of courage with her famous ancestor.

Noor was good at keeping secrets. Noor's family were often in danger. Sometimes they did not always tell people that they were royalty in order to keep themselves safe. This made Noor think very carefully about what she told others about her life. Keeping secrets was going to be a key spying skill for Noor!

a gold, jewelled tiger head, which once decorated Tipu Sultan's golden throne

A preacher and musician

Noor's father, Hazrat Inayat Khan, was a classical musician and also a **Sufi** Muslim preacher. Hazrat's teachings were about peace and tolerance. He left India to share his passion for Indian classical music and spread his religion to western countries. This was how he met Noor's mother, Ora Ray Baker, when he was lecturing in San Francisco in the US.

Sadly, things did not go smoothly for Hazrat Inayat and Ora. Both of their parents were unhappy because they didn't feel that people with different religions and races should get married. Hazrat and Ora ignored their parents and got married all the same!

Baby Noor

Hazrat and Ora married in London. The couple were then invited to Russia to preach and play music.

Noor was born in a monastery in Moscow, Russia, on 1st of January 1914. Her father and mother, or "Abba" and "Amma", named her Noor-Un-Nisa Inayat Khan. This name meant "light among women". When Noor was 40 days old, a joyful ceremony was held to welcome her at her parents' home.

Soon the family grew and Noor became the big sister to two brothers, Vilayat and Hidayat, and a baby sister, Khair-Un-Nisa.

Difficulties in England

When Noor was eight months old, her family left Russia and went back to London where they continued to spread their Sufi religion and Indian classical music.

Unfortunately, life was hard because they were poor, and Noor's father, Hazrat, found it difficult to find a job. Sometimes, Noor and her brothers and sister only had bread to eat, and often went hungry.

Noor with her brother Vilayat and father Hazrat Inayat Khan

11

Learning to speak French

After a few years in London, the family decided to move to France. Hazrat continued to preach Sufism and share Indian classical music there.

Although it was another big change for Noor, she would spend much of her life in Paris, and she came to adore the city. At the age of eight, Noor started school.

pupils in a classroom in 1922

It was a challenge because she did not speak French. Noor was different from the other schoolchildren and faced racism. However, her determination helped her cope and she learned to speak French. Noor's knowledge of French ended up benefiting her. It was because she spoke French so well that she eventually got her job as a spy!

Creative Noor

In Paris, Noor lived in a special house, called
the Fazal Manzil or "The House of Blessing".
This house was a centre for religious teaching.
It was a grand house surrounded by a walled
garden filled with trees. You could even see
the lights of the city and the Eiffel Tower in
the distance. Among its many rooms, the house
had a music room where Noor learned to play
the **veena**, the harp and the piano.

In 1927, when Noor was just 13 years old,
the family had a terrible shock. Noor's beloved
father, Hazrat, died unexpectedly. Noor's mother
never really recovered from her husband's death,
and as a result, Noor became responsible for
her family. Even though she was still very young,
she took on more housework, and looked after
her mother, brothers and sister.

Noor with her family at Fazal Manzil, the "House of Blessing"

Noor enjoyed making up stories for her siblings, in order to keep them entertained and happy. The creativity Noor showed when making up these stories also helped her cope with her own sadness.

Noor the writer

When Noor was in her twenties, some of her children's stories were **published**. One of her friends was a children's illustrator, and she suggested that Noor should **translate** some Indian stories about the religious teacher, **Buddha**. Many of these stories were about courage and self-sacrifice. Little did Noor know that she would soon need these very same qualities when she became a spy …

War begins

When the Second World War began in 1939
Noor was 25 years old. Her life in Paris changed
beyond belief. The war was started by Adolf
Hitler, the German leader, who wanted to
rule all of Europe. Britain and France fought
against Germany. Hitler and his followers were
called Nazis.

THE Washington Times

WAR IN EUROPE!

The Nazis **persecuted** Jewish people and they passed laws that made it harder for Jewish people to live a safe, normal life. For Noor, these laws went against the deeply-held belief in peace and freedom that she had grown up with. She found Hitler's persecution of Jewish people personally painful because she was now engaged to be married to a Jewish music student.

Noor the nurse

Noor was determined to help defeat Hitler, and so she and her sister, Khair, both began training as nurses with the French **Red Cross**. The two sisters wanted to look after French and British soldiers who had been injured in the fighting. They worked in a hospital near to the fighting and even refused to leave when the combat got really close!

They were eventually **evacuated** because they were in danger, as the German army was so close. During her time as a nurse, Noor was already proving herself as a person who made courageous decisions and was not afraid of danger. These skills and strong qualities became crucial when she was a spy!

A nurse's work

Below are some examples of the sort of tasks Noor and Khair might have carried out while working as Red Cross nurses:

- first aid – for example, bandaging a wound or making a sling for a broken arm

- bedmaking and cleaning

- washing patients who couldn't move

- serving food and refreshments

- talking and playing games with patients to help them feel better and keep them distracted from their pain

- helping patients regain movement after they had been injured.

A Red Cross nurse in Paris
during the Second World War.

Stay or go?

Noor was now 26 years old. By June 1940, most of France – the country she loved and had lived in since she was six – was occupied. This meant it had been taken over by the Nazis. It was only a matter of time before the Nazis took over Paris as well.

Noor's mother's health had worsened. So, it was up to Noor and her brothers and sister to decide whether they should leave their beloved childhood home, Fazal Manzil, or stay.

Millions of people fled Nazi-occupied France in 1940.

Noor and her family decided that in order to keep themselves safe they would leave France as quickly as possible and go to England. Fortunately, they made the right decision by leaving, because just nine days after they had escaped, the German army occupied Paris and took control of the city. Between 8 and 10 million **refugees** fled France around the start of the Nazi occupation. Noor vowed to return to Paris as soon as she could. Until then, however, she was determined to do everything she could to stop the Nazis from winning the war.

A difficult journey

Noor's brother, Hidayat, had a car, and he drove the family as far as the town of Tours in the west of France. The journey was very difficult because many places they passed through had already been burnt or bombed by the German army and many roads had been destroyed.

When the family finally reached the town of Tours, they said a final farewell to Hidayat, who had decided to stay behind in France. The rest of the family boarded an extremely crowded train.

Hidayat later moved to the south of France with his wife and children, and joined the French resistance. This was a group of men and women who fought against the Nazi occupation.

The family, without Hidayat, planned to go to Bordeaux, near the east coast of France. From there they would catch a boat to England, where they would be safer.

However, when they got to Bordeaux the town was so busy with refugees that no one was let off the train. Noor's family were stuck, unable to leave the train and get the boat to England. Luckily, their journey wasn't over.

Last boat

The train continued for 50 more miles until it reached the little coastal town of Le Verdon. There was panic as hundreds of people tried to board the last few boats sailing to England. Luckily, because Vilayat – Noor's brother, was born in London, he was a **British citizen**. This meant that Noor's family were able to get a precious place on a boat.

Noor and her family were part of a plan by the British Government to evacuate thousands of troops and civilians from ports in western France to England. The boat Noor was sailing in was under constant threat of being bombed by Nazi aircraft.

Noor's family had a crowded and dangerous journey in a boat that was designed to carry **cargo** rather than people.

The boat was overrun with beetles and there was no room for any luggage because so many people were jammed onto the boat.

As Noor and her brother looked back at France, they resolved to return as soon as possible and help free France from Nazi occupation. The family were very relieved to have made it to safety when they arrived in Falmouth on the English coast.

part of the evacuation of troops and refugees in 1940

Could you be a nurse?

Could you be a nurse for the Red Cross?
Check and see if you have the key skills needed
for the job!

Nurses need to be able to:

- be friendly with other nurses and with
  their patients

- be trustworthy so that patients know that they
  can rely on them to help

- have an eye for detail to avoid any mistakes

- be able to adapt, you never know what a day
  might bring

- work as team to get the job done!

29

Chapter 3 Spy school

Joining the fight

Once they arrived in England, the family separated again. They each found a way to help fight the war against the Nazis.

Vilayat travelled to London and joined the Royal Navy, whose military ships protected Britain's coastline. Vilayat worked on a minesweeper which was a navy ship that detected and exploded enemy bombs that were hidden in the sea.

Noor was delighted to be doing more to help win the war by joining the **WAAF**, the "Women's Auxiliary Airforce". At the interview she pretended her name was Nora Baker as she thought this would make it easier for her to fit in with her new British work friends.

Like Vilayat, she started her training by detecting enemy bombs. She watched a special **radar** screen which showed when German aircraft were about to drop bombs nearby.

Women in the WAAF used these special screens to detect nearby enemy planes!

Noor learns Morse code

Over the next year, Noor was chosen to specialise as a radio operator. She learned to send and receive messages using Morse code, which was a way of sending information over long distances. It worked by tapping long and short sounds out over the radio.

Each sound combination was equivalent to a letter and so messages were sent by spelling out words. For example, a short sound followed by a long sound was the code for the letter "A".

Noor tapped the Morse code keys so loudly, she was teased by her friends, who called her "Bang Away Lulu!" This didn't stop her though, and by the time she had finished her training she was the fastest radio operator in England.

Spy school recruit

The Nazis now occupied much of France, and
Noor wanted to do even more to help win the war.
She was interviewed in order to get a better job
in the British army. Noor felt confident in her
skills and wanted to look smart for her interview.
So, she borrowed one pound from her brother,
Vilayat, and had her hair done in the latest style.
The questions she was asked were difficult, but
Noor answered truthfully.

Noor's army bosses realised that she might make a good spy in France, particularly as she spoke fluent French. So Noor had another interview, but this time it was kept secret. In order not to be found out, it didn't take place in a smart army building, but in a scruffy London hotel room. The curtains were kept drawn and her interviewer wore a suit rather than a uniform. No one would have suspected that a spy interview was taking place!

Noor in the SOE – Special Operations Executive

Noor was thrilled to be recruited as a spy for the top-secret organisation called the Special Operations Executive (SOE). The SOE was very important. It was set up by the Prime Minister of Britain, Winston Churchill, himself.

Winston Churchill

The SOE aimed to:

- spy on the enemy and collect information about their numbers and whereabouts

- make it harder for the enemy to rule the countries they occupied, including France – for example, by blowing up bridges or trucks full of weapons. This was known as **sabotage**.

Noor was part of the SOE "F Section", that organised spying in France. Only 39 of the 470 agents sent to France were women.

Spy school

When Noor started her training, she no longer wore an army uniform, but khaki clothing that made her look like a nurse rather than a spy. She had to promise to keep everything she learned a secret by signing an agreement called the **Official Secrets Act**.

Noor trained in various secret locations to become a spy. She excelled in key aspects of the role, including Morse code, and her tutors were impressed by her hardworking nature.

However, Noor struggled with other parts of her training, and it was noted that she was clumsy and scared of using weapons. Noor may have found using weapons difficult because she held peaceful beliefs – she would only use them as a last resort to defend herself. The physical aspects of her training were challenging. For example, although she could run, she found climbing difficult and wasn't allowed to learn to parachute because she found it tricky to land on her feet!

Noor's spy report

Noor's final training was in the village of
Beaulieu in Hampshire. She needed to pass
a test which involved travelling by herself
to a city 80 miles away. Once there, she had
to find a house that was safe to hide in and
transmit a message in Morse code.

She needed to use a fake identity and do all this while avoiding being followed. Her teachers checked everything, including making sure that she didn't talk in her sleep as she might give herself away to the enemy.

Her teachers disagreed about whether Noor would be a good spy. Some thought it unlikely because she was too gentle, unathletic and emotional. They were worried that if she was captured by the Nazis, she would give away too many secrets.

However, the head of the training school thought Noor had the right character, a positive attitude and would make a brave spy.

So, in 1942, Noor made her final preparations to go to France and spy on the Nazis.

Morse code

A	• —		S	• • •
B	— • • •		T	—
C	— • — •		U	• • —
D	— • •		V	• • • —
E	•		W	• — —
F	• • — •		X	— • • —
G	— — •		Y	— • — —
H	• • • •		Z	— — • •
I	• •		0	— — — — —
J	• — — —		1	• — — — —
K	— • —		2	• • — — —
L	• — • •		3	• • • — —
M	— —		4	• • • • —
N	— •		5	• • • • •
O	— — —		6	— • • • •
P	• — — •		7	— — • • •
Q	— — • —		8	— — — • •
R	• — •		9	— — — — •

Can you work out this message in Morse code?

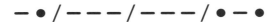

Can you spell out a secret message in
Morse code by tapping out the code with
your fingers on a table? You could type one
of the following words:

Help

Hide

Run

Radio secrets

The plan was for Noor to be the first female radio operator to go to France. She would use a Mark 2 radio that weighed about 15 kilograms (or the weight of three small cats) that would need to be kept hidden in a suitcase. The radio needed an **antenna** to work which needed to be placed somewhere high up, like on a roof. It could send a signal over 500 miles to Britain. Noor learned how to send radio messages by creating her own secret code. She even used her favourite poetry phrases to help her create secret codes which were impossible for the enemy to crack.

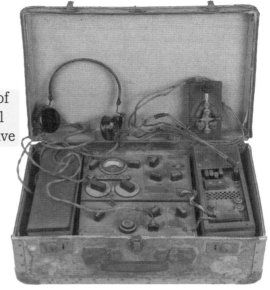

the Mark 2 radio of the British Special Operation Executive

Family secrets

At Beaulieu, Noor was reminded of the dangerous nature of her mission. She understood that she might not return. She was prepared to risk her life in order to win the war and fight the injustice of the Nazi occupation. However, Noor worried about her mother who was very distressed at having to leave France. Her mother was also struggling with the loss of her husband, as well as the violence of war, which clashed with her peace-loving beliefs.

Noor shared her worries with her boss, Vera Atkins. They decided not to upset her mother and Noor lied, pretending she was leaving to work in Africa.

Vera Atkins

Pills and disguises

When Noor arrived in Paris she would be disguised as a French nurse. In order to be believable, Noor had her hair styled and her clothes made in a French style. Every detail was thought about. Her bosses even removed the English labels on her clothes and replaced them with French labels.

Noor was also provided with a number of secret pills. One could be put in the tea or coffee of an enemy, and would make them drowsy. Another was a pill that would help Noor stay awake. These pills would be considered unsafe today but were vital during wartime.

Codename Madeleine

Noor had a fake identity which she needed to remember at all times.

Some parts of Noor's fake identity were like her real life. For example, as we know, her father had really died when she was young. These similarities helped make her fake identity more believable.

Given that Noor had a total of four names at this point, it would have been easy for her to get confused. Remember, her British colleagues knew her as Nora Baker, not by her real name, Noor. She also had her spy name, Jeanne-Marie Renier, and her code name, Madeleine!

the name Noor would
use in France

TOP SECRET
DESTROY AFTER READING

Name: Jeanne-Marie Renier

Job: Children's nurse

Birthday: 25th April 1914

Father's job: a professor who died
in the First World War

Codename: Madeleine

the name Noor would use in her radio
messages to Britain and with other
SOE agents and resistance fighters

Spy plane

On the night of 16th June 1943, Noor made
the dangerous journey to France. Her boss
helped her check she had nothing that might
give her away to the enemy – something as
simple as an English bus ticket could prove fatal.
Vera pinned a silver bird to Noor's clothing and
wished her luck. The plane was tiny with no
weapons, navigation systems or lights. Flying to
France by moonlight was the safest option.

The landing site was in a field and was lit
up by torches. The SOE agents and resistance
fighters waiting in France used Morse code to tell
the pilot it was safe for them to land. Noor made
a bumpy landing back on French soil, but there
was no time for her to adjust to the shock of being
in France again. In fact, in a matter of minutes
the plane was reloaded and took off with injured
and frightened people escaping the war.

Noor's plane

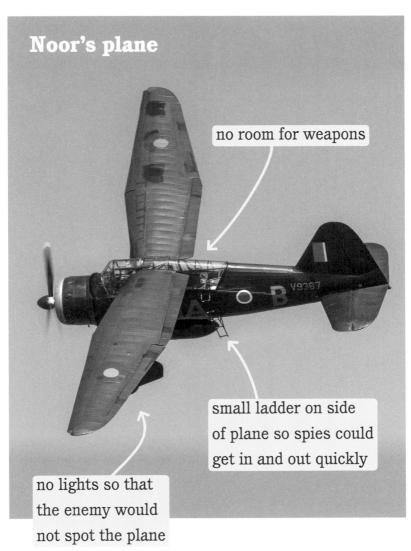

no room for weapons

small ladder on side
of plane so spies could
get in and out quickly

no lights so that
the enemy would
not spot the plane

Brave women

Noor was the first female radio operator to be flown into France.

The chances of being caught by the enemy were very high for radio operators because they had to carry their radios with them. Most radio operators were expected to survive only six weeks before they were captured or killed.

On the plane that evening were two other women who were also working as spies in France. Cecily Lefort, who had trained with Noor, and Diana Rowden.

It meant everything to Noor to be able to keep her promise to return to France and help defeat the Nazis.

In the next chapter, you will find out what Noor did in France and how long she managed to stay undercover for before she was captured. Can you guess? Do you think it was longer than six weeks – which was the average length of time that radio operators survived in France? Clue: Noor was a brilliant spy.

Noor in her SOE uniform, in 1943

Noor's fake ID

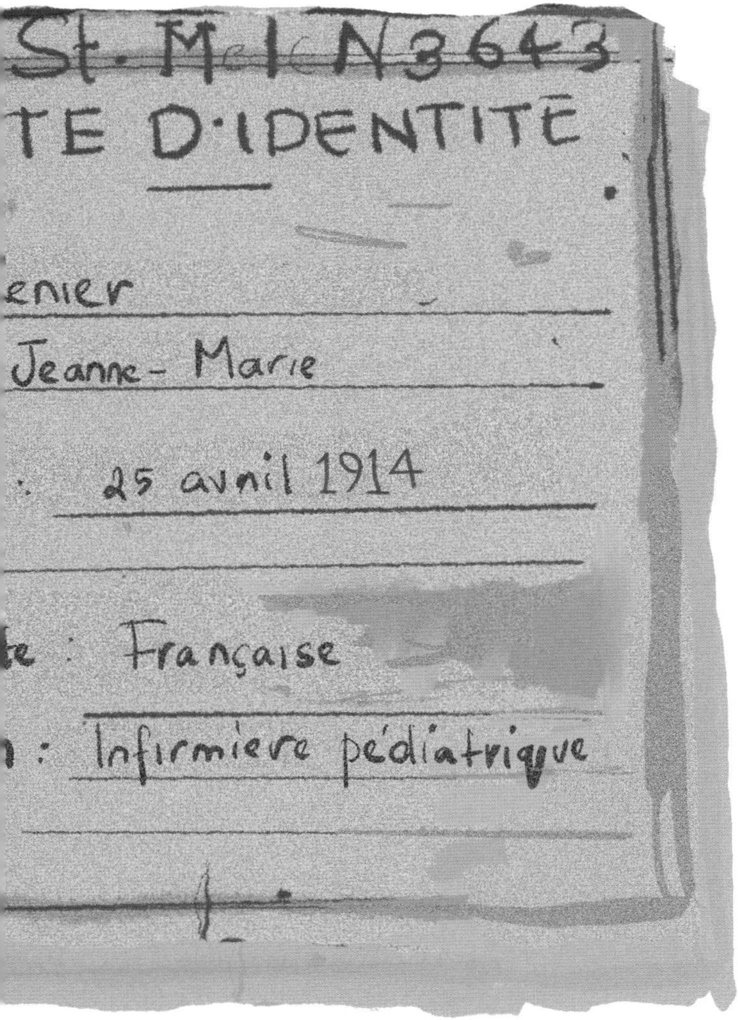

St. M-I-N3643

TE D'IDENTITÉ
___

enier

Jeanne - Marie

: 25 avril 1914

te : Française

: Infirmière pédiatrique

Spy suitcase essentials

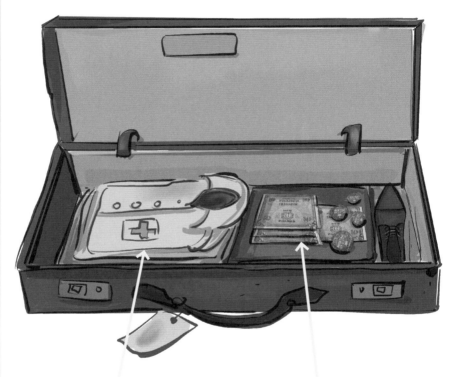

nurse uniform   french money

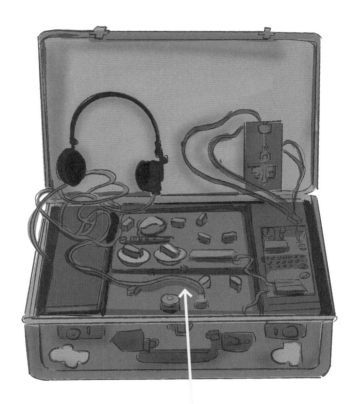

radio

Chapter 5
Noor's last stand

A very different Paris

After landing, a nervous Noor biked alone by moonlight to the railway station and then caught a train to Paris. When she arrived, she was devastated by what she saw. Nazi flags flew over all the government buildings and Nazi soldiers were everywhere. There were shortages of food, energy and clothing, and Parisians had to stay indoors at night.

Noor realised that she would need to keep moving so that she wasn't captured. She played the part of Jeanne-Marie Renier, as she had been trained to do, by speaking French and pretending to be a nurse.

Clothes drop

As there was no room on the plane which transported Noor to France, her radio and clothes were dropped off by parachute a few days later. Luckily, her radio was not damaged.

Noor was worried her clothes might give her away as a spy, as people might be suspicious of them lying in the field. So, she arranged for them to be recovered as quickly as possible.

Once Noor got her radio, she sent her first message back to Britain. She used her codename "Madeleine" and indicated that she'd arrived safely.

Betrayal

Within a few days of Noor's arrival in France, disaster struck. Six radio operators were arrested by the Nazis. Later, it was discovered that one of the spies who had met Noor's plane was a double agent. This meant he pretended to work as an SOE agent while also working for the Nazis and betrayed the SOE agents to the Nazis.

Things did not improve for Noor after this disaster. She was going for a meeting at the spy headquarters, which was hidden in a school that taught farming.

As she was cycling towards the location, Noor had a "gut" feeling something was wrong and she changed direction. Later, she discovered that the Nazis had arrested all the spies at the school. Noor was now the last radio operator left in Paris.

An amazing spy

When her bosses in London realised that Noor was on her own, they asked her to return immediately to Britain for her own safety.

Bravely, she decided to stay.

Noor managed to keep transmitting for over three months before she was captured. She did the work of six people.

In order to keep operating alone for such a long time, Noor used all her spy skills when sending messages to London. She was always on the move, never living in one place for too long.

She hid her radio in lots of ways. She used shopping bags and even a baby's pram.

She was always ready to use her cover story. Once she was stopped and questioned by a Nazi officer about what was in her suitcase.

She didn't say it was her radio – instead she said she had "cinematographic apparatus" (a way of describing film equipment). The officer did not know what this was and let her pass.

Living among the enemy

Noor kept hidden by changing her appearance.
She dyed her hair different colours, wore wigs
and changed her clothes.

Noor's messages helped the French resistance
fight the Nazis. She sent information about
weapons and money. She helped other spies enter
and leave France.

She even saved the lives of resistance fighters
and troops who needed to escape. Noor was
also able to tell Britain about spies who had
been captured.

As time passed, the enemy was getting better at finding radio operators. They had vans with technology that could find operators who sent messages for more than 15 minutes. So Noor kept her messages to just 5 minutes long.

Once, Noor moved to a flat in a building that she did not realise was full of Nazis.

One night, Noor needed to send a message. She wanted to hang her radio antenna from a tree and was very surprised when a Nazi officer offered to help her hang it.

Noor had to think very quickly. She told the officer that she wanted to listen to jazz music on the BBC radio. She confessed that although she knew radios were forbidden, she loved listening to jazz.

The officer believed her and helped her hang the antenna on the tree, before wishing her "goodnight" and leaving. She then transmitted her message to Britain right under the Nazis' noses.

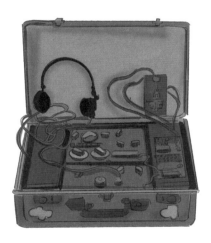

The months of being the only radio operator were exhausting. It wasn't surprising that Noor made a mistake by leaving some of her secret information in one of the places she was staying.

The Nazis found her notes and discovered that her codename was "Madeleine". Noor did not realise this, but from then on, the Nazis were desperate to capture the mysterious Madeleine. As a result of finding her secret information, they were able to capture more agents and get closer to Noor.

Two Nazis pretending to be SOE officers tried to trick Noor into meeting them in a café. Luckily, as Noor approached the meeting place, she realised something was wrong and escaped once again.

After another close escape, Noor realised that she could no longer do her job and sent a message to London asking to be flown home.

Spy gadgets

False footprints:
Spies would wear these rubber soles underneath their shoes, to disguise their footprints.

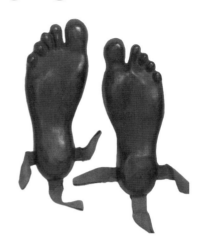

Photographer pigeons:
Small cameras would be attached to a pigeon's chest. These cameras would take hundreds of photos while the pigeon flew!

Spy cameras: These tiny cameras were designed to be as small as possible, so that they could be hidden anywhere!

Spy torches: Spies would have to be ready for anything, even at nighttime! These torches were small enough to hide in a pocket.

Chapter 6 Capture

A friend's betrayal

Noor was alone in Paris and decided she couldn't leave France before seeing her old friends and visiting her childhood home. She managed to say goodbye to some friends, but this was her worst mistake. One friend told the Nazis where she was living in return for a lot of money.

When Noor returned to her flat, she was captured. She fought hard but was outnumbered. One of the Nazis described her as an angry "tigress", just as her great-great-great-grandfather, Tipu Sultan, had been described as a "tiger". She had been just a few hours away from returning safely back to England by plane.

Noor's escape attempts

Even after she was captured, Noor did not give up. She tried to escape twice.

Immediately after her arrest she was taken to a special building used by Nazis to question SOE agents. When Noor arrived there, she asked to use the toilet. The bathroom door was left open with a brick to stop prisoners from escaping.

Noor charmed the guard into removing the brick to let her use the bathroom in private. She then escaped through the bathroom window and walked along the guttering on the outside of the building. She was on the fifth floor, and despite her bold attempt, the guards soon discovered her.

74

A daring plan

Noor still didn't give up. When she heard another prisoner in the cell next door, she made contact by tapping out Morse code on her cell wall. She and the other prisoner decided to try and escape.

They managed to steal a screwdriver and loosen the windows in each of their cells. Noor even demanded face powder from her guard and then used the face powder to cover the holes around the windows!

In the dead of night, the prisoners climbed out of their windows onto the roof. Unfortunately, there was an **air-raid warning**, and this meant the guards checked on all the prisoners. Desperately, the prisoners climbed down from the roof using knotted bed sheets.

Noor kicked in the glass window of one of the rooms in the storey below and ran down the stairs. Unluckily, the soldiers were already waiting outside the building and immediately captured Noor and the other prisoner.

Liberty

The Nazis decided that Noor was a "highly dangerous" prisoner. She was the first female agent to be transferred to a German prison and was labelled as "return not required" which meant that they never intended to release her. She never betrayed her friends or her colleagues and refused to help the Nazis. Noor was killed by the Nazis on 13th September 1944, when she was just 30 years old.

It is believed that her last word was "*liberté*" which means "freedom" in French.

Her boss, Vera Atkins had the heart-breaking job of telling Noor's family and friends about what had happened to her.

Although Noor died, her bravery will always be remembered.

Noor's awards

Immediately after Noor died, she was given many awards.

At a remembrance ceremony in Paris, one of the speakers talked about Noor's heroic acts. They commented that even though Noor's background and religion made her different from many people in France and Britain she still chose to fight.

Maybe, now we have learned more about Noor, we might think it was *because* of Noor's difference – her beliefs and her traditions – that she wanted to fight injustice.

Just as she was taught by her father, Noor always tried to help others. She ultimately died fighting for peace and justice.

French military medal,
Croix de Guerre, awarded
for acts of heroism

the George Cross,
Britain's highest civilian
award for gallantry

A forgotten hero

After the war, Noor's bravery and the bravery of many other SOE agents, particularly women, began to be forgotten. A few people did not want this to happen and fought hard to have Noor and other women remembered in a more permanent way.

So, in 2012, 67 years after the end of the war, a statue of Noor was unveiled in Gordon Square, London, which was where Noor used to live.

Queen Elizabeth the Second also unveiled a memorial remembering Noor in St Paul's Cathedral in London.

In the past, it was mostly men who were remembered in history for what they achieved. But how we think about history is changing. Noor's statue shows that now we remember the acts of great women too.

NOOR
INAYAT KHAN
1914-1944
G.C., M.B.E.
Croix de Guerre

Unveiled by
HRH The Princess Royal
on 8 November 2012

Princess Anne and Shrabani Basu,
Noor's biographer, unveiled the statue
in Gordon Square.

A blue plaque

A blue plaque is used in England to mark
a building where someone important lived.
Noor was honoured with a blue plaque
at her wartime home, 4 Taviton Street,
Bloomsbury, London. She scratched this address
on a bowl when she was in prison so that people
would know who she was.

Noor was the first woman of a south Asian
background to be honoured with a blue plaque.

Now that you have read Noor's story, is there anything in this picture of Noor as a young woman that hints at her amazing spying abilities? She was a small, imaginative, unathletic girl who grew up to change our ideas about who could be a successful spy. Her courage, loyalty and determination made her an exceptional person. Like Tipu Sultan, her great-great-great grandfather, she could not bear the injustice of occupation and was prepared to die for this ideal.

Noor really was a "light among women" because her actions shone through her fight for freedom for all, regardless of race or religion.

Glossary

air-raid warning an alarm to warn people when an attack by military aircraft, is expected

antenna a device, often a wire, that sends and receives television or radio signals

British citizen a person or child of a person who was born in Britain or a British territory

Buddha the title given to Gautama Siddhartha, the religious teacher and founder of Buddhism

cargo the goods a ship or plane is carrying

colonise to go to another country, live there and take control of it by force

evacuated sent to a place of safety

Official Secrets Act an act of Parliament that covers the protection of information relating to state security

persecuted when someone is treated cruelly by others, often because of their race or beliefs

published to have printed copies of books or magazines to be sold

radar a way of using radio signals to discover the position of aircraft or ships

Red Cross an international organisation that helps people who are suffering, for example as a result of war, floods or disease

refugees people who have been forced to leave their homes or their country, either because of war or their political or religious beliefs

sabotage to deliberately damage something, for example, a railway line or a bridge, in a war

Sufi Muslims who are very focused on spiritual learning

translate to be heard or read in one language and then repeated in a different language

veena an Indian stringed musical instrument

WAAF the Women's Auxiliary Airforce, formed during the Second World War, to assist the Royal Air Force

About the author

How did you get into writing?
I loved making up magical stories for my younger cousins. They lived in India and I lived in England. Because this was a time before computers, I used to write down my stories in letters which I would post!

Ayesha Braganza

What do you hope readers will get out of the book?
I hope that readers will try to do things that might at first seem impossible.

Is there anything in this book that relates to your own experiences?
I was an imaginative child who wasn't good at sport – maybe there is still time for me to be a spy! (Or maybe I am already a spy, but not a very good one as I've just told you!)

What is a book you remember loving reading when you were young?
The Magic Faraway Tree by Enid Blyton. I loved all the wonderful characters like Moon-Face and I wanted different magical lands to appear at the top of my favourite tree just like in the book.

What is it like for you to write?

It was so interesting and so much fun finding out about Noor – and sad too – because she died so young. It's amazing that she believed in fighting injustice at any cost.

Why did you want to write this book?

My friend introduced me to Noor's story a few years ago and I became hooked.

What was it about Noor's story that interested you?

I loved the fact that she was a person of colour who was a real heroine during World War Two. When I was growing up, I didn't know that people of colour were important in British History.

Would you want to be a spy yourself?

I would like to be a spy, but I don't think I'd be very good at keeping secrets or being without my family and friends like Noor did. I wouldn't be brave enough to hide my radio in a baby's pram and walk past the Nazis officers – I would be too scared! Though, maybe if my way of life and the people I love were threatened, perhaps I would find unexpected bravery inside myself.

What kind of research did you have to do for this book? Did you enjoy it?

Yes, I did a lot of interesting research. I even read some of the stories Noor wrote for children like: *The Monkey Bridge* about a very brave King Monkey who sacrificed himself to save his followers – a bit like Noor did.

About the illustrator

A bit about me ...

I am Fathima, an architect turned artist from India.

Fathima Hakkim

What made you want to be an illustrator?

Art allows me to be my authentic self without the fear of making mistakes. And creating art feels like pure magic to me.

How did you get into illustration?

I started drawing when I was just 4 years old, and I haven't stopped. Becoming an illustrator felt like an impossible dream for someone like me in my society. But I kept at it, drawing every day and eventually I was on the road to being an illustrator.

What did you like best about illustrating this book?

I enjoyed studying Noor's life closely and bringing her to life. It was an absolute honour to give life to her in my imagination.

Is there anything in this book that relates to your own experiences?

I relate to Noor with her cultural background and her daring mind to do something that was so challenging. I love challenges as they help me evolve and grow as a person. I can also relate to her passion for justice, her confidence and intelligence.

How do you bring a character to life in an illustration?

First, I research and learn about them, I immerse myself in their stories and try to view their world from my own perspective. I put myself in their shoes and try to think like they would.

Did you know about Noor before you illustrated this book? What do you think of her?

I read about Noor when I was young and I thought she was incredibly brave. She inspired me and showed that anyone can do anything if they put their soul into it.

Would you like to be a spy yourself?

I personally think I would give away that I am a spy because I have an expressive face, and I would have "I am a spy" written all over it!

Book chat

What did you know about World War Two before reading this book?

What was the most interesting thing you learned from reading this book?

Had you heard of Noor Inayat Khan before reading this book?

If you had to give the book a new title, what would you choose?

What do you think were Noor's best qualities?

What do you think are the most important skills for a spy to have?

What did you know about spies before reading this book?

What surprised you most about the life of spies during World War Two?

Book challenge:

Design your own spy gadget.

Collins
BIG CAT

Published by Collins
An imprint of HarperCollins*Publishers*
The News Building
1 London Bridge Street
London SE1 9GF
UK

Macken House
39/40 Mayor Street Upper
Dublin 1
D01 C9W8
Ireland

© HarperCollins*Publishers* Limited 2023

10 9 8 7 6 5 4 3 2

ISBN 978-0-00-862487-3

British Library Cataloguing-in-Publication
Data

A catalogue record for this publication is
available from the British Library.

Download the teaching notes and
word cards to accompany this book at:
http://littlewandle.org.uk/signupfluency/

Get the latest Collins Big Cat news at
collins.co.uk/collinsbigcat

Author: Ayesha Braganza
Illustrators: Fathima Hakkim
  & Roger Stewart (Beehive Illustration)
Publisher: Lizzie Catford
Product manager: Caroline Green
Series editor: Charlotte Raby
Development editor: Catherine Baker
Project manager: Emily Hooton
Commissioning editor and
  content editor: Daniela Mora Chavarría
Copyeditor: Sally Byford
Proofreader: Gaynor Spry
Typesetter: 2Hoots Publishing Services Ltd
Cover designer: Sarah Finan
Production controller: Katharine Willard

Collins would like to thank the teachers and children at the
following schools who took part in the trialling of Big Cat
for Little Wandle Fluency: Burley And Woodhead Church of
England Primary School; Chesterton Primary School; Lady
Margaret Primary School; Little Sutton Primary School;
Parsloes Primary School.

Printed and bound in the UK by Page Bros Group Ltd

MIX
Paper | Supporting
responsible forestry
FSC™ C007454

Acknowledgements
The publishers gratefully acknowledge the permission
granted to reproduce the copyright material in this book.
Every effort has been made to trace copyright holders and
to obtain their permission for the use of copyright material.
The publishers will gladly receive any information enabling
them to rectify any error or omission at the first opportunity.

p7 incamerastock/Alamy, pp12–13 Penta Springs Limited/
Alamy, p21 /AFP/Getty Images, p22–23 Sueddeutsche
Zeitung Photo/Alamy, p27 Trinity Mirror/Mirrorpix/Alamy,
p29 Eddie Gerald/Alamy, p31 piemags/Alamy, p36 World
History Archive/Alamy, p45 INTERFOTO/Alamy, p46
GL Archive/Alamy, p51 Kev Gregory/Shutterstock, p55
IanDagnall Computing/Alamy, p70t © IWM, p70b Science
History Images/Alamy, p71t © IWM, p71b © IWM, p79l
agefotostock/Alamy, p79r PjrStudio/Alamy, p81 LEON
NEAL/AFP/Getty Images, p82 ISABEL INFANTES/AFP/Getty
Images, p83 Pictorial Press Ltd/Alamy.